THE AMAZING RISE OF
JEREMY LIN

UNDER DOGS

SPORTS CHAMPIONS

★ ★ ★

★

★

BY MARTIN GITLIN

45TH PARALLEL PRESS

Published in the United States of America by Cherry Lake Publishing Group
Ann Arbor, Michigan
www.cherrylakepublishing.com

Reading Adviser: Beth Walker Gambro, MS, Ed., Reading Consultant, Yorkville, IL
Series Adviser: Virginia Loh-Hagan
Book Designer: Jen Wahi

Photo Credits: cover: Abaca Press/ Alamy Stock Photo; page 5: © DvYang, CC BY-SA 2.0, via Wikimedia Commons; page 7: © Matthew Emmons/USA TODAY Sports; page 9: © zhangjin_net/Shutterstock; page 13: © Hilary W Berkowitz/The Harvard Crimson; page 15: Mike D, CC BY-SA 2.0, via Wikimedia Commons; page 17: Jeremy_Lin_against_Warriors.jpg: nikk laderivative work: Bagumba, CC BY 2.0, via Wikimedia Commons; Page 21: © Matthew Emmons/USA TODAY Sports; page 25: David Shankbone, CC BY 3.0, via Wikimedia Commons; page 29: © zhangjin_net/Shutterstock

Copyright © 2024 by Cherry Lake Publishing Group

All rights reserved. No part of this book may be reproduced or utilized in any form or by any means without written permission from the publisher.

45th Parallel Press is an imprint of Cherry Lake Publishing Group.

Library of Congress Cataloging-in-Publication Data

Names: Gitlin, Martin, author.
Title: The amazing rise of Jeremy Lin / written by Martin Gitlin.
Description: Ann Arbor, Michigan : 45th Parallel Press, 2023. | Series:
  Underdogs. Sports champions | Audience: Grades 4-6 | Summary: "The
  Amazing Rise of Jeremy Lin takes readers inside the unexpected NBA
  career rise of Jeremy Lin during his 2011-2012 season with the New York
  Knicks. Provides background leading up to Lin's mega-popularity, review
  of the season, why the world was shocked, and what happened afterward.
  From players no one believed in to teams no one thought could win,
  Underdogs: Sports Champions covers some of history's greatest underdogs.
  Written in a strong narrative nonfiction style, the storytelling in
  these books will captivate readers. The series includes considerate
  vocabulary, engaging content, clear text and formatting, and compelling
  photos. Educational sidebars include extra fun facts and information"--
  Provided by publisher.
Identifiers: LCCN 2023005885 | ISBN 9781668927786 (hardcover) | ISBN
  9781668928837 (paperback) | ISBN 9781668930304 (ebook) | ISBN
  9781668931783 (pdf)
Subjects: LCSH: Lin, Jeremy, 1988---Juvenile literature. | Basketball
  players--United States--Biography--Juvenile literature.
Classification: LCC GV884.L586 G579 2023 | DDC 796.323092
  [B]--dc23/eng/20230216
LC record available at https://lccn.loc.gov/2023005885

Cherry Lake Publishing would like to acknowledge the work of the Partnership for 21st Century Learning, a network of Battelle for Kids. Please visit http://www.battelleforkids.org/networks/p21 for more information.

Note from publisher: Websites change regularly, and their future contents are outside of our control. Supervise children when conducting any recommended online searches for extended learning opportunities.

Printed in the United States of America
Corporate Graphics

★

★

TABLE OF CONTENTS

Introduction

What makes sports fun? Fans love watching sports. They love watching great athletes. They love seeing the best in action. They're awed by their skills. They're awed by their talent.

But what makes sports interesting? One never knows what will happen. Fans can expect an outcome. Their side could win. Or their side could lose. Nobody knows for sure.

Sometimes an upset happens. An upset is when a team that's expected to win loses. Upsets make fans sad. They confuse people.

Sometimes an underdog rises to the top. Underdogs can be players. They can be teams. They have little chance of winning. Yet, they win.

Jeremy Lin tries out his jump shot in a game against the L.A. Lakers on February 10, 2012.

Surprises happen. They're shocking. But they're wonderful. They're fun to watch.

That's why games are played. That's why fans watch games. They don't know who's going to win. They don't know who's going to lose. This is the point of sports. Not knowing is exciting.

Upsets in sports are legends. Legends are great stories. They're remembered forever. Underdogs make people smile. They inspire. They give hope. There are many sports champions. The most loved are underdogs. This series is about them.

photo: © Matthew Emmons – USA TODAY Sports

Jeremy Lin gets fouled in a game against the Dallas Mavericks on March 6, 2012.

Warming Up

People are often judged too quickly. That's not right.

Jeremy Lin is a basketball star. But many doubted him. They judged him before meeting him. They judged him without knowing him. They never thought he'd be an NBA star. NBA is the National Basketball Association. It's a professional basketball league.

Lin wasn't like other great basketball players. He wasn't tall. He wasn't big. He didn't look strong. His parents were from Taiwan. Asian American players in the NBA are rare.

Few really knew Lin. They didn't know his drive. They didn't know his love for the game. They didn't see his skills. But they learned many years later.

首钢

7

林书豪

Many people doubted Jeremy Lin at the start of his career. They learned how wrong they were years later.

Lin grew up in Palo Alto. Palo Alto is in northern California. Lin learned basketball from his father. He showed some talent. But that's not why he excelled. Lin has passion. He worked hard.

He wanted to be great. And by high school, he was. He was a guard. Guards pass the ball. Lin could pass the ball. But he could also shoot. He was great at playing defense. Defense means stopping the other team from scoring.

Lin was also a great team player. He led his high school to a 32–1 record. This means his team won 32 games. Lin's team became state champions. He was named the top player of his division. He had proven himself.

But college coaches judged him. They didn't see Lin as a star. Lin had to fight to be seen.

When he went to high school, Jeremy Lin was just 5-foot-3. But he grew. By senior year, he was 6-foot-3. He could do everything on the court. One of his best skills was dribbling. Dribbling means bouncing the ball. Lin dribbled to the hoop. He moved in position. He could shoot or pass the ball. This resulted in easy baskets. He set his team up to score points. As a senior, he scored 15 points per game. He made about 7 assists per game. Assists are passes that lead to points. He made about 5 steals. Steals mean taking the ball away from the other team. He made more than 6 rebounds per game. Rebounds mean getting the ball after it misses the hoop. Lin also studied hard. He had a 4.2 grade point average. That means he got all A's. He was a top student.

The Upset

College scouts recruit the top athletes. They didn't care to see Jeremy Lin play. They didn't offer him scholarships. Scholarships are money used to pay for college. They attract players to attend schools.

Lin applied to many colleges. He sent tapes of himself playing. He showed his talent to top basketball programs. Among them were Stanford and UCLA. (UCLA is the University of California Los Angeles.)

He was mostly ignored. But he was a great student. So, he got into top academic colleges. Academic schools are more interested in grades. They also gave him a chance to play basketball.

Lin decided to attend Harvard University. Harvard is one of the top universities in the United States. It's part of the Ivy League. This is a group of top U.S. private schools.

By the end of his time playing for Harvard University, Jeremy Lin was scoring more than 16 points per game.

Lin moved to Massachusetts. He traveled across the country. He wanted to show off his basketball talent. But it took time. In his first year, he scored about 5 points per game. His coaches needed him to get stronger. One called him the weakest player.

Lin knew that. So he worked harder. He got better. And so did his numbers. He became a star. In his second year, he scored nearly 13 points per game. In his last 2 years, he scored more than 16 points per game.

Lin set many Ivy League records. He was the first player with 1,450 points. He was the first player with 450 rebounds. He was the first player with 400 assists. He was the first player with 200 steals. But that wasn't good enough. Every NBA team ignored him. They all passed on him in the 2010 draft. In a draft, teams select the top college players.

Lin had to promote himself. He had faith. He earned tryouts with several teams. Tryouts are like tests. Lin did a great job. He was invited to join the Golden State Warriors.

He went back home. He returned to California. But he rarely played. Soon the Warriors let him go. This was very upsetting. Some players might have given up. But not Lin. He knew he could play in the NBA. And he was going to prove it.

Jeremy Lin lines up with the Golden State Warriors before warming up for a game. He played with the Warriors for the 2010–2011 season.

The Shocker

Lin was without a basketball team. The 2011 season had begun. He worked on his game. He gained 15 pounds of muscle. Yet no team reached out.

Finally, the Houston Rockets did. But 12 days later, they let him go. Then he signed with the New York Knicks. They needed a guard. But he was just filling out a roster. Rosters mean the players on a team. Lin rarely played. He was a backup.

It's not cheap to live in New York. Lin didn't have a place to stay. He slept on his brother's couch. This was not ideal. He didn't know if basketball was working out.

Soon he was sent to the D-League. This is where players prepare for the NBA. It's a lower level. Lin couldn't wear an NBA uniform. But he'd be able to play. He did well. Coach

David Lee of the Golden State Warriors is unable to block Jeremy Lin from taking a jump shot at this 2011 game.

Mike D'Antoni was the Knicks' coach. He needed some good luck. His team was failing. He gave Lin a chance. Three days later, the Knicks brought Lin back.

D'Antoni didn't regret it. Lin was amazing. He scored 25 points. He had 7 assists. The Knicks beat New Jersey. Their winning streak had begun. They beat Utah. Lin scored 28 points. He had 8 assists. The Knicks beat Washington. Lin scored 23 points. He had 10 assists. The Knicks beat the Los Angeles Lakers. Lin scored 38 points. He had 7 assists. On and on it went. There was one great game after another. Lin turned the Knicks into a winning team. They won 7 straight games. Lin was in the starting lineup. This meant he played when the game began.

Lin was a super thief. He stole the ball a lot. This made the other team mad. He made almost 2 steals per game on average.

New York fans loved him. His greatness shocked the basketball world. It seemed as if he came out of nowhere. He got a lot of attention. He got a lot of cheers. His amazing rise was given a name. It was called "Linsanity." It was insane how good he was.

Linsanity didn't last long. But it was okay. Lin found his place in the NBA. He proved what he knew all along. He could be a star if given a chance.

SAME SPORT, DIFFERENT STORY

The Cleveland Cavaliers played in the NBA Finals. They lost the finals in 2007 and 2015. But they had another chance. The year was 2016. It looked as though they were going to lose. They had lost 3 of the first 4 games. One more defeat, and it would be over. They didn't want to lose again. They played against the Golden State Warriors. The Warriors had beaten them the year before. There'd be no shame in losing to the Warriors. The Warriors had won 73 games that season. It was the best record in league history. But the Cavaliers had a superstar. Their superstar was LeBron James. James and Kyrie Irving went to work. Winning wouldn't be easy. No team had ever won Finals while down 3–1. The Cavaliers were expected to lose. They had to win Game 5. They did that. Then they had to win Game 6. They did that. Game 7 arrived. The game was tied. There was less than a minute left. Irving made a long shot. That basket gave Cleveland the victory. It was the Cavaliers' first title.

The Crowd Goes Wild

It was early February 2012. Everybody had a case of Linsanity. Even U.S. President Barack Obama. Obama watched Lin play on TV. He saw him beat Toronto. One second was left. Lin hit a shot. That gave the Knicks a win. Obama called Lin's rise a "great story."

Everyone was talking about Lin. He was the first Asian American star in the NBA. But it was more than that. Lin's numbers were amazing. He scored about 23 points. He made 9 assists. He did this over 11 games. He led the Knicks to a 9–2 record. He made half his shots. He was a great player.

Lin was a big deal. He became famous. His number 17 jersey became the top seller. Jerseys are the players' shirts. Sales exploded.

photo: © Matthew Emmons – USA TODAY Sports

Jeremy Lin fights Lamar Odom to drive to the basket in a game against the Dallas Mavericks on March 6, 2012.

Mike D'Antoni was thankful. Lin had turned his team around. D'Antoni recalled how Linsanity took over. He said, "It was the greatest time ever. It caught fire. So fast and unexpected." He talked about what it was like "at the Garden." He's talking about Madison Square Garden. That's where the Knicks play their home games. Linsanity brought life to the Garden. The fans were wild for Lin. This made the games more exciting. It pumped up the team. D'Antoni said, "There's nothing better than that, other than winning a championship."

In 2012, Linsanity was the biggest sports story. Even *TIME* magazine thought so. It put Lin on its "100 Most Influential People" list. Lin was praised for his grit. He was also praised for paving the way for other Asian American players. (There were other Asian American players. But Lin was the first to get treated like a rock star.) *TIME* wrote, "Jeremy Lin's story is a great lesson for kids everywhere . . . He achieved success the old-fashioned way. He earned it. He worked hard and stayed humble. He lives the right way. He plays the right way."

Lin continued to play the right way. But the winning streak stopped. Linsanity ended before the end of the season. But it was an amazing ride. Lin made his mark.

★ Jeremy in is a TV star! He had a small part in *Fresh Off the Boat*. He has starred as himself many times. In 2022, HBO made a film about Linsanity. It's called *38 at the Garden*.

★ Lin is in a music video. The video is called "The First Opponent." Opponent means someone who competes against you. He worked with MC Jin. MC Jin is an Asian American rapper.

★ Lin is proud of his Asian heritage. He took Mandarin classes at Harvard. (Mandarin is a Chinese language.)

★ Lin donates money. He's given 1 million dollars to help those affected by COVID-19. He's also spoken out against anti-Asian hate.

★ Lin loves playing video games. His favorite is *Defense of the Ancients 2* (*DOTA 2*). He's in *Free to Play*. This is a movie about the game. He has his own *DOTA 2* team. The team is called J. Storm.

Moving On

It was March 14, 2012. It was 5 weeks after Linsanity started. But times had changed. Lin was still playing well. But the Knicks were not. They had lost 6 straight games.

The coach is blamed when a team falls apart. So the Knicks forced Mike D'Antoni to quit. D'Antoni was replaced by Mike Woodson. The team then started to win. The Knicks played better. But Lin did not. He missed most of his shots. He still passed the ball well. But his scoring totals dropped.

Lin didn't score at all after late March. He had a knee injury. He stopped playing. He had to get surgery. Surgeries are when doctors perform operations. They fix injuries. It takes time to heal.

Jeremy Lin even made *TIME* magazine's "100 Most Influential People." Linsanity will never be forgotten.

Linsanity had ended. But Lin's career was still going strong. He no longer fit in with the Knicks. So he played with the Houston Rockets. He signed a 3-year contract.

Lin didn't mind that the attention was over. He focused on being a good player. He didn't shoot the ball as much. But he was still a great passer. He racked up assists. He kept stealing the ball.

He helped the Rockets reach the playoffs. Playoffs are a series of games. They determine an NBA champion.

That's when his struggles began. He played poorly in the first round. He had a chest injury. This forced him to sit out 2 games. His career was never the same.

He stayed in the NBA until 2019. He bounced from team to team. But Lin still loved to play. He decided to play overseas. He went to China. He signed with the Beijing Ducks.

★
★

Jeremy Lin made an impact through basketball. He changed the way people saw Asian Americans. Many did not see them as athletes. Linsanity changed their minds. Lin was an Asian American athlete. He was also a star. He was winning games. He was famous. Crowds chanted his name. But he struggled as a child. He wanted to play basketball. But he lacked Asian American role models. (Lin was the fourth American-born NBA player of Asian heritage. Others were Wataru Misaka, Raymond Townsend, and Rex Walters.) He said, "Society has always tried to say Asians can't do this. Asians can't do that . . . What [Linsanity] meant was just being able to compete on the same court, in the same arena. And then to defeat and to overcome and to win." He wants people to fondly remember Linsanity. But he also hopes everyone gets an equal chance to play.

He played well. He scored about 22 points per game. He nearly won Defensive Player of the Year. This happened in 2020.

But Lin wanted to prove himself again in the NBA. He returned to the Warriors. He was sent to Santa Cruz. That is where its G-League team played. The G-League is the NBA's official minor league. (It's the new name for D-League. It's named after Gatorade. Gatorade sponsors it.)

Lin played great in 9 games. Yet the Warriors didn't add him to the NBA team. So, he returned to China. He signed with the Guangzhou Loong Lions. This happened in 2022. Linsanity was a distant memory. But those amazing months would never be forgotten.

★ Before playing for the Guangzhou Loong Lions and the Kaohsiung Steelers, Jeremy Lin played for the Beijing Ducks.

Learn More

Books

Doeden, Matt. *Coming Up Clutch: The Greatest Upsets, Comebacks, and Finishes in Sports History*. Minneapolis, MN: Millbrook Press, 2018.

Gitlin, Marty. *Jeremy Lin: Basketball Phenom*. North Mankato, MN: Sportszone, Abdo, 2012.

Yorkey, Mike and Jesse Florea. *Linsanity: Kids Edition*. Nashville, TN: Zonderkidz, 2012.

Explore These Online Sources with an Adult:

Britannica Kids: National Basketball Association

Jr. NBA

Sports Illustrated Kids: NBA

Glossary

academic (ak-uh-DEM-ik) Relating to school and schoolwork

assist (uh-SIST) A pass of the ball that directly leads to a basket

defense (DEE-fens) The action of stopping the opposing team from scoring

D-League (DEE LEEG) The development league for basketball players where they prepared for the NBA (former name of G-League)

draft (DRAFT) An event during which NBA teams select top college players

dribbling (DRIB-ling) The skill of using one hand to continuously bounce the ball on the court

G-League (JEE LEEG) The NBA's official minor league basketball organization (named G for Gatorade, the sponsor)

guard (GAARD) A player often responsible for passing the ball and scoring

Ivy League (IYE-vee LEEG) A group of long established colleges and universities in the eastern United States having high academic and social prestige

jersey (JER-zee) The uniform shirt that players wear as part of a team

legend: An extremely famous story that is told many times

NBA (EN BEE AY) National Basketball Association, a professional basketball league in North America

opponent (uh-POH-nent) Someone who competes against you, a rival

playoffs (PLAY-awfs) Games played to determine an overall champion

rebound (REE-bownd)When a player gets the ball after it misses the hoop and has a chance to score

roster (RAH-ster) Players that make up a team

scholarship (SKAH-ler-ship) Money given by a school to cover tuition, used to lure athletes to play for that school

scout (SKOWT) A person who helps recruit the best athletes

starting lineup (STAR-ting LYNE-up) An official list of the players who will participate in the event when the game begins

steal (STEEL) A turnover that happens when a defensive player takes or intercepts the ball from the opposing team

surgery (SERJ-ree) A procedure to fix an injury or other physical problem

Tryout (TRIE-owt) A test of the potential of someone to determine a place on a team

underdog (UHN-der-dawg) A player or team that has little chance of winning but ends up winning

upset (UHP-set) When the team that is expected to win loses

Index

About the Author

Martin Gitlin is a sports book author based in Cleveland. He won more than 45 awards as a newspaper sportswriter from 1991 to 2002. Included was a first-place award from the Associated Press for his coverage of the 1995 World Series. He has had more than 200 books published since 2006. Most of them were written for students.